HOW TO BEE PROSPEROUS

A Bee devotional by Sheila Textor

ISBN: 978-1-7361575-0-3
Independently published by Sheila Textor

First edition, 2020.

Book designed and edited by: Sinclaire Sparkman

Blytheville, Arkansas

www.beebiblesmart.com

YouTube: Sheila's One Stop

HOW TO BEE PROSPEROUS

Table of Contents

Introduction

Let's be real with one another. We all want to prosper in some form. Some of us look for ways to bring more money into our lives, while others seek influence. Often we search for a place of recognition and honor in our community. As Christians, prosperity comes to us in more ways than money.

In this book you will find 31 days of devotionals each including a scripture, explanation, prayer, and two journaling questions with space to write. These scriptures and insights will encourage us to hold to the word of God, because no matter the season you are in you can prosper and have great success.

My dear friends, it is God's great pleasure to bless and prosper his people. This 31-day devotional is loaded with Biblical truths that will have your expectation at a whole new level. When you take action to learn these simple principles, your life will never be the same again. The Bible says God does not lie. Get ready for doors of prosperity to open up on your journey as you glean from this devotional prayer journal.

Day 1
Joshua 1:7–8

7 Only be thou strong and very courageous, that thou mayest observe to do according to all the law, which Moses my servant commanded thee: turn not from it to the right hand or to the left, that thou mayest prosper whithersoever thou goest. 8 This book of the law shall not depart out of thy mouth; but thou shalt meditate therein day and night, that thou mayest observe to do according to all that is written therein: for then thou shalt <u>make thy way prosperous</u>, and then thou <u>shalt have good success</u>.

Underline added by me for emphasis.

These scriptures are rich with gold nuggets. They have a guideline that we can follow that guarantees us a prosperous life.

God is instructing Joshua on how to remain under the same success that Moses had. We may look at Moses and think he sure took the long way around to leading the people to the promised land. He was their human deliverer from Egypt, and he would be their guide for many days and even years.

Moses failed at keeping his cool, and that cost him from crossing over into the natural promised land. One thing he had, though, was a divine connection with God. God must have seen him as a leader with a heart for the people.

The Word of God is our guide. The Bible is our book full of riches untold. God tells Joshua if he won't turn to the right hand or the left hand—in other words stay on the path that has been laid out—then whatever he does will prosper.

Prayer:
God of the universe, I am looking to you. You are the way, the truth and the light. Help me today to stay on the path you have chosen for me. I know my success is different from yours sometimes. I want to prosper in every area of my life. I want success in my home, in my business and mostly in the church. God, my success may look different than others, but help me to learn your Word so that I have knowledge to move only in the direction you want me to go.

Call to Action:

What does success mean to you?

_____

_____

_____

_____

_____

_____

_____

_____

_____

_____

_____

_____

_____

_____

_____

_____

_____

_____

What does meditating on His Word mean to you?

_____

_____

_____

_____

_____

_____

_____

_____

_____

_____

_____

_____

_____

_____

_____

_____

Day 2
Proverbs 10:22

The blessing of the LORD, it maketh rich, and he addeth no sorrow with it.

Notice that the blessing has no 's' on the end of it. This simply means it stands alone in its meaning.

When we can get the blessing, other things fall into place as well. The blessing comes from that connection with our maker, and that connection means that no matter what is going on there is peace and contentment in your soul.

There is a richness that has nothing to do with money. To be rich in God is to be knowledgeable of His Word, to have wisdom, knowledge, and understanding, which are priceless gems in the Kingdom of God. These three aspects of life are like having acres of diamonds. With these three tools in your work belt you can attain natural riches. You can own land, own buildings, and own property. You can make wise investments with steps ordered by the Lord.

Seek His guidance for your next step, your next purchase, your next investment. I have sought God all through my writing journey, with my networking skills and connection with Him.

No matter what you have set out to do in your life, God has ways to bring abundance into your endeavors and prosper you beyond your wildest dreams.

Prayer:
God, I ask you to bless me with your blessing. I ask that you bring the wealth of the sinner to the righteous. I don't ask for riches to show off. I ask for your blessing so I can turn around and bless others. I can give more. I can help the helpless and the poor. God, through your Word I'm learning how to grow in wisdom, which is a priceless gem. Wisdom and connection can bring many great things into my life. Your word compares wisdom to rubies. God, I want all you have for me. But show me how and what to do with the gifts you have bestowed on me.

Call to Action:

What blessing would you like to see God bring into your life? There is no right or wrong answer.

_____

_____

_____

_____

_____

_____

_____

_____

_____

_____

_____

_____

_____

_____

_____

_____

_____

_____

What would you do with the Lord's blessing?

_____

_____

_____

_____

_____

_____

_____

_____

_____

_____

_____

_____

_____

_____

_____

_____

_____

Day 3
Deuteronomy
28:1–14

Two of the 14 verses are printed. Feel free to look up the whole passage and read it. Each verse in this passage is laced with treasures to dig up and packed with blessings that almost seem beyond our human minds.

1 And it shall come to pass, if thou shalt hearken diligently unto the voice of the LORD thy God, to observe and to do all his commandments which I command thee this day, that the LORD thy God will set thee on high above all nations of the earth:
2 And all these blessings shall come on thee, and overtake thee, if thou shalt hearken unto the voice of the LORD thy God.

Consider the word *shall*.

This word is not a guessing word; it's a promise of something that is going to happen. Diligently means to care about your actions, to do something with much delight and care.

If we will take great thought to how we live our lives for God, and how our hearts are turned toward His ways, we will see the blessings of God overtake us. It takes intention to live in line with His commandments and receive His blessings.

This passage is one of my go to passages for decrees and declarations.

We are the head and not the tail.

Prayer:
God, I am one of your children. I need your heavenly wisdom to help me do the right thing. Help me, God, to diligently hearken to your voice. Even more, help me to know your voice. I look for blessings when I have obeyed your commandments. Help me as a human to understand that as I walk in your ways that it is beneficial for my life even here on earth. I want to see the goodness of the Lord in the land of the living.

Call to Action:

As you read this and ponder on it, what is a declaration that you would like to declare today and stand on it through this passage?

_____

_____

_____

_____

_____

_____

_____

_____

_____

_____

_____

_____

_____

_____

_____

_____

_____

_____

_____

How can you hearken diligently unto the voice of the Lord each day?

_____

_____

_____

_____

_____

_____

_____

_____

_____

_____

_____

_____

_____

_____

_____

_____

_____

Day 4
Deuteronomy 29:9

Keep therefore the words of this covenant, and do them, that ye may prosper in all that ye do.

This passage is short but powerful.

Sometimes we're looking for some big event, some great swelling words to be spoken over us. God spoke to Elijah in a still small voice, which speaks loudly to us through this small but significant verse. We expect the thunder and lightning, but God only wants us to do the next right thing.

Keep the words of His covenant and prosper. A covenant is like agreement to do what is in a contract or even marriage. Look into what God expects from us. Since this is a small devotional, I don't have the space or time to teach on His expectation for His people. All of us, though, can get a sense of right and wrong. You do what is right and honorable and you will prosper.

To prosper can mean many different things. A person prospers when God gives wisdom to make sound decisions in the affairs of life. Peace, strength, and courage are all part of heavenly prosperity.

Mostly anyone wants to prosper in monetary things as well. There is a quote that is very fitting for this reflection, if we continually give, we will continually have.

Prayer:
Heavenly Father, I ask for understanding of your covenant. I want to keep my side of the covenant, so I will see God's hand in every area of my life. I need guidance in my everyday affairs. I ask that you show me favor and prosperity through your Word and my agreement to keep my end of the contract (so to speak). Lord, this scripture is short but carries a big punch. Help me to not only know your commandments, but to do them, that everything I do will prosper. Thank you Father for hearing my sincere pleas.

Call to Action:

What do you think a covenant means in this passage?

_____

_____

_____

_____

_____

_____

_____

_____

_____

_____

_____

_____

_____

_____

_____

_____

_____

_____

Write down anything you may improve on in your walk that might open up more blessings in your life.

_____

_____

_____

_____

_____

_____

_____

_____

_____

_____

_____

_____

_____

_____

_____

Day 5

Psalm 35:27

Let them shout for joy, and be glad, that favour my righteous cause: yea, let them say continually, Let the LORD be magnified, which hath pleasure in the prosperity of his servant.

I love this verse. Many times as Christians we feel like we shouldn't be looking for prosperity. In this reading, though, we find God taking pleasure in our prosperity. Why wouldn't He? God has given us guidelines and instructions to be prosperous.

When I was young, I always felt like seeking to be wealthy in this life was in contest with seeking pure things of God. And I do believe that we shouldn't seek only the wealth of this world, yet God promises us this blessing as a reward (so to speak) for doing the right thing. I believe as a child of God if we obey His Word and walk upright before Him, we should have expectation of His blessings, however they come.

We are His children, and He compares His heart of giving to our hearts as parents. We as parents want to give our children good gifts, though those gifts can be a moral insight or a new car for graduation.

It's not so much what it is, it's the desire, the longing to want the best for them, and we have the power sometimes to fulfil those needs or wants. There is another scripture nestled even in this reflection; we'll take a look at it in the next devotion.

Prayer:
God, I am fleshly, so even though I seek a godly walk and vision, I also look forward to God's favor and rewards for the acts of obedience. I want to love and serve you first and foremost and thank you for your love and mercy toward us. I also stand on the Word, knowing that you are a good God and Father and you truly want me to benefit from the promises in your Holy Bible. I thank Him now for His rich blessings He has in store for His children.

Call to Action:
How would you like God to prosper you, spiritually and naturally?
List what you would do with those requests when they are granted.

_____

_____

_____

_____

_____

_____

_____

_____

_____

_____

_____

_____

_____

_____

_____

_____

_____

_____

_____

_____

Would you say that you favor God's righteous cause?

_____

_____

_____

_____

_____

_____

_____

_____

_____

_____

_____

_____

_____

_____

_____

Day 6
Psalms 84:11

For the LORD God is a sun and shield: the LORD will give grace and glory: no good thing will he withhold from them that walk uprightly.

What a promise! No good thing will He withhold from us if we walk upright before Him.

A "good thing" can mean many different things to each person. To one person, a good thing may be a house; to another, it may be a good paying job. A good thing can also be having needs met with a nice fat bank account. Or it can be many things together. Even as you read this reflection, you may have a good thing in your mind.

I don't believe God expects us to be perfect. I do believe He requires us to do the Christian thing. When we know right from wrong and we choose to do the right thing, God pays attention.

Many Christians may see a modest dress code as walking upright. Many may see it as not lying or cheating or stealing, etc. Each person has to ask God for direction in situations that we face daily. Walking upright is also keeping our hearts and minds in a peaceful and non-judgmental attitude.

I have seen God bring many good things into my life, simply because I chose to do the right thing.

Prayer:
Dear God, help me today to walk upright before you, not just to gain your blessings, but also to put forth a good example. I am extremely thankful for your goodness. Everyday I am faced with decisions between right and wrong. I will listen to your voice. It can be so simple sometimes, just choosing not to gossip or to let someone have our parking space. God, your promises far outweigh our light afflictions. Thank you for all the good things you have placed in my life.

Call to Action:

What is something good that has happened to you because you feel like you did the right thing?

_____

_____

_____

_____

_____

_____

_____

_____

_____

_____

_____

_____

_____

_____

_____

_____

_____

_____

How can you be sure that your values align with God?

_____

_____

_____

_____

_____

_____

_____

_____

_____

_____

_____

_____

_____

_____

_____

_____

_____

Day 7
Psalm 118:24–25

24 This is the day which the LORD hath made; we will rejoice and be glad in it. 25 Save now, I beseech thee, O LORD: O LORD, I beseech thee, send now prosperity.

"This is the day the Lord hath made," look at this verse. How many times have we quoted this? I have said it many, many times. How many times have we quoted the next verse?

I don't remember if I have ever said it out loud. But in this passage, it seems like the writer is expressing how soon he wants God to bless him. We all have probably been there. Immediate needs come up in life. Lord, we need thee now.

Beseech means to ask someone urgently and fervently to do something. No doubt, David needed God to show up in a way that made his enemies realize that God was on his side. Send now prosperity.

I feel like God moved quickly for David. He had the courage to nudge God to move quickly. We may not be David, but we are God's workmanship, and He wants to bring prosperity into our lives.

I am prone sometimes to think if I struggle I am more spiritual. My dear friends, I would challenge you to dig in the word of God and find the real truths about God's attributes, especially with prospering His children.

Prayer:

God, I beseech you, move for me quickly. Bring prosperity into my life. I will use the blessing wisely. I know your Word encourages me to believe that you want to bless me. I also pray that you only bring what I can handle. Help me to know that not all of us can handle well the prosperity that God truly wants for his children. I will unselfishly give of my gain to those in need. God, we see that not all people have this revelation that you want to see your children blessed. I recognize that my struggle does not make me more spiritual. Only you, God, can make that happen. Draw me closer to you, Lord.

Call to Action:

How do you feel about asking God to prosper you quickly?
Why do you feel that way?

_____

_____

_____

_____

_____

_____

_____

_____

_____

_____

_____

_____

_____

_____

_____

_____

_____

_____

How were you taught about prospering?

_____

_____

_____

_____

_____

_____

_____

_____

_____

_____

_____

_____

_____

_____

_____

_____

_____

Day 8

Zechariah 8:10–12

10 For before these days there was no hire for man, nor any hire for beast; neither was there any peace to him that went out or came in because of the affliction: for I set all men every one against his neighbour. 11 But now I will not be unto the residue of this people as in the former days, saith the LORD of hosts. 12 For the seed shall be prosperous; the vine shall give her fruit, and the ground shall give her increase, and the heavens shall give their dew; and I will cause the remnant of this people to possess all these things.

At the writing of this devotional, there is chaos in our country. We are dealing with both Covid-19 and the death of an African American by the hands of a white cop. There are protests being held all over our country, which brings the opportunity for some to steal and more killings.

This passage talks about a dark time as well, especially verse 10. Everyone was against each other. Let's look at verse 12: even in the midst of trouble, God is telling them they will prosper. The vine will give her fruit. The ground shall give her increase. He will cause the remnant to possess all these things. What a wonderful promise to know that God will bless and keep you even in the darkest hours.

The remnant are the ones who hold on to God, lift up the blood stained banner, and live as Holy as they can.

Hold on to Bible truths, my dear friend, and watch God bless you.

Prayer:
Dear heavenly Father, help me today to hold on to your promises, to stand for you no matter what others are doing or not doing. Thank you for assurance that you have me covered. It's your desire for me to prosper and succeed. Thank you for blessing me in these uncertain times. Show me how to stay connected to the source of strength and power that will allow me to be counted as part of the remnant so I can possess all the blessings you have stored up for me.

Call to Action:

Do you remember a dark time? Do you think God was taking care of you through that time?

_____

_____

_____

_____

_____

_____

_____

_____

_____

_____

_____

_____

_____

_____

_____

_____

_____

_____

_____

How were you feeling during this dark season?

_____

_____

_____

_____

_____

_____

_____

_____

_____

_____

_____

_____

_____

_____

_____

_____

Day 9

Psalm 122:6–7

6 Pray for the peace of Jerusalem: they shall prosper that love thee. 7 Peace be within thy walls, and prosperity within thy palaces.

Sometimes we can see big things in small verses.

Looking at our scripture for today, we see a direction on what to pray when we need prosperity. Praying for the peace of Jerusalem brings prosperity to the city. In saying our prayers for peace, we will have prosperity within our palaces, our lives, if you will.

By looking at these examples of prosperity we see that the Bible is full of promises and blessings that are for His children. Why wouldn't we want what God has for us?

Peace is a priceless commodity. I wouldn't trade my peace for a million worlds and all their riches. Prosperity can look different to each of us. But peace allows us to have a respect for whatever prosperity God wants to give.

Setting our mind on worry instead of peace could forfeit the natural prosperity, so let's pray for peace for Jerusalem and the palaces in our lives.

Prayer:
God, I pray for peace for Jerusalem and in my own life. I will prosper if I love my fellow man. I will have peace and prosper-ity within my walls. I want what you have for me. I will seek your face and your righteousness, so that I can be an example to my fellow believers. I will pray for the abundant life that you said I could have. I will not back up because others seem to judge people that look for natural blessings. Your Word says you have come to give us life and that more abundantly. I'm seeking the things of God. I will not be ashamed to stand on your promises of blessing your people.

Call to Action:

How do you see this passage?

_____

_____

_____

_____

_____

_____

_____

_____

_____

_____

_____

_____

_____

_____

_____

_____

_____

_____

_____

_____

How would you like God to bless you, even in the natural?

_____

_____

_____

_____

_____

_____

_____

_____

_____

_____

_____

_____

_____

_____

_____

Day 10
Isaiah 55:10–11

10 For as the rain cometh down, and the snow from heaven, and returneth not thither, but watereth the earth, and maketh it bring forth and bud, that it may give seed to the sower, and bread to the eater: 11 So shall my word be that goeth forth out of my mouth: it shall not return unto me void, but it shall accomplish that which I please, and it shall prosper in the thing whereto I sent it.

This is one of my declarations that I have written down in my prayer journal. I love the way it compares our words to rain and snow.

Speaking accomplishes things we don't always see with our natural eyes. Sometimes the rain we get in one season will provide nourishment in the next season. God's word does not return void.

The words that are coming out of your mouth are planting for a season to come. They will prosper in where you send them.

Speak the promises of God over your life. If your words are going to prosper, if they are going to manifest, then desire the goodness of God to produce. Send your thoughts/ words toward good things to manifest in your life.

Prayer:
God, I will speak over my circumstances. Your words are life. Your words are true. I thank you that I'm able to understand that my words will manifest and prosper where I send them. I will speak with power and knowledge of your promises, that if I walk upright before you, you will not withhold any good thing from me. My words have power and they will open the windows of heaven for me and pour me out a blessing I can't contain. My words are like the snow and rain, they come now and sometimes manifest later in another season. I will reap a harvest of the goodness of God.

Call to Action:

Do you speak over your life with God's promises?

_____

_____

_____

_____

_____

_____

_____

_____

_____

_____

_____

_____

_____

_____

_____

_____

_____

_____

_____

_____

Will you start declaring God's promises today? What would you declare first?

_____

_____

_____

_____

_____

_____

_____

_____

_____

_____

_____

_____

_____

_____

_____

_____

_____

Day 11

Deuteronomy 30:14–16

14 But the word is very nigh unto thee, in thy mouth, and in thy heart, that thou mayest do it.15 See, I have set before thee this day life and good, and death and evil; 16 In that I command thee this day to love the LORD thy God, to walk in his ways, and to keep his commandments and his statutes and his judgments, that thou mayest live and multiply: and the LORD thy God shall bless thee in the land whither thou goest to possess it.

I challenge you to read this whole chapter, especially verse 11 and down. It tells us that our desire to receive God's blessings or His provision is not beyond us. It is not hidden from us.

As humans, we can sometimes feel like God is way out there and really doesn't concern himself with our natural desires. He simply is giving us a choice to choose life or death or good or evil.

Many may say, "I didn't choose evil to come into my life." I'm well aware that there are things that come into our lives that we have no control over. I also believe that sometimes our actions or decisions to involve ourselves with people are choices we make on our own, and that can bring unwanted actions to our life. But this passage is letting us know it's nigh at my mouth.

You can speak the things you want to see manifest in your life. You can prosper, even in the natural. Speak blessings and do not lack.

Prayer:
Heavenly Father, help me to speak with wisdom about my life. Help me to choose wisely. Help me to obey your commandments and keep your statutes that I may live and multiply. I know that prosperity is not beyond me, that it's nigh in my mouth. My choices today will affect my tomorrows. I know that the children of Israel were possessing a natural land, but you let us know that we can possess territory, rather that territory be real land or buildings or just wisdom to speak with knowledge of our future. I'm so in love with your plan for us and how you show us how to be prosperous people. It's nigh at my mouth.

Call to Action:

How will you talk now that you know God's promise for prosperity is nigh at your mouth?

_____

_____

_____

_____

_____

_____

_____

_____

_____

_____

_____

_____

_____

_____

_____

_____

_____

_____

What do you want God to manifest in your life?

_____

_____

_____

_____

_____

_____

_____

_____

_____

_____

_____

_____

_____

_____

_____

_____

_____

Day 12
Isaiah 3:10

Say ye to the righteous, that it shall be well with him: for they shall eat the fruit of their doings.

The full chapter of Isaiah 3 shows that God will reward unrighteousness as well as righteousness. Rather, if you sow to the good or the bad, you will eat the fruit of your doings.

I can you tell that I have not always sown to the good. I have sown seeds that I had to pray for God to show mercy on for their harvest. By no means am I some great spiritual giant now, I just learned a few lessons the hard way. My goal now is to make sure if I'm gonna eat the fruit of my doings, I definitely want it to be sweet and wholesome.

Our doings can be many things. Being faithful to God and man, giving time and possessions, sowing good things such as these will bring back great dividends in life. Who doesn't want to prosper in this life?

Let's sow and reap prosperity on the journey to meet Jesus. Let's make sure that the things we do are the things that please God and that our harvest is sweet to the taste and not bitter.

Prayer:
Oh God, show me the way I need to go. Show me the things I need to be doing, that it will be well with me. I want sweet fruit. Good and juicy fruit. I want the things to which I put my hands to be prosperous. I want to be a righteous person. If I fall short, remind me who you are and that it's in my hands to bring the goodness of the Lord into my life. Righteous simply means to do right. I will do the right things that I can see the hand of God distinguishably upon my life.

Call to Action:

What does *righteous* mean to you?

_____

_____

_____

_____

_____

_____

_____

_____

_____

_____

_____

_____

_____

_____

_____

_____

_____

_____

If you eat the fruit of your doings, would your fruit be sweet or bitter?

_____

_____

_____

_____

_____

_____

_____

_____

_____

_____

_____

_____

_____

_____

_____

_____

_____

Day 13

Proverbs 13:21–22

21 Evil pursueth sinners: but to the righteous good shall be repayed. 22 A good man leaveth an inheritance to his children's children: and the wealth of the sinner is laid up for the just.

Again we see that good shall be repaid.

I want to hone in on verse 22. Inheritance will look different to different people. Some may think of the spiritual. Some may think of land or possessions, money or anything of value. I feel like it's a little of all of it.

My parents left me nothing: no money, no land and really no kind of spiritual blessing either. I'm sad that I just became aware of this passage and even it's natural meaning. My children know about God; they know how to pray; they know how to live a righteous life. But, what I'm doing now, I should have done years ago.

I want to leave them a business, a path where they can pick up the reins and continue on with building wealth in all areas. I am aspiring to leave them with a legacy. I want my books to bring them income and other benefits even after I'm gone from this life.

The wealth of the sinner is laid up for the just. The just is the people that are living a righteous life. The ungodly will lay up for us. I've seen this time and time again.

I have seen the sinner give to God's people hand over foot. God's word doesn't lie. We should expect the goodness of God everyday.

Prayer:
Dear Father, help me to make wise decisions. I want to leave inheritance to my children and grandchildren. Help me God to show my children and grandchildren a lasting inheritance. I want them to know God in all his power, but I also want to leave something that will last for generations. I want God to show me ways to invest myself and my time into things that will carry on for years. I want to see my grandchildren continue in the work of God as well as in the natural things.

Call to Action:

What does leaving an inheritance for your children look like to you?

_____

_____

_____

_____

_____

_____

_____

_____

_____

_____

_____

_____

_____

_____

_____

_____

_____

Have you ever seen the sinner give to God's people?

_____

_____

_____

_____

_____

_____

_____

_____

_____

_____

_____

_____

_____

_____

_____

_____

Day 14

Genesis 39:21–23

21 But the LORD was with Joseph, and shewed him mercy, and gave him favour in the sight of the keeper of the prison. 22 And the keeper of the prison committed to Joseph's hand all the prisoners that were in the prison; and whatsoever they did there, he was the doer of it. 23 The keeper of the prison looked not to any thing that was under his hand; because the LORD was with him, and that which he did, the LORD made it to prosper.

We can't do a devotional without Joseph. He is one of my favorite examples in the Word of God.

He didn't ask for God to put him in this place. He was chosen, though. Honestly, we are all chosen to do a work for God. Some people will live their whole life and never really step into that work.

Many times when God begins to show up in our life and begins to deal with our hearts to go a certain way, we are all excited until the first resistance shows up, then we begin to question if it was God or our own desires. Either way, we see Joseph sharing his dreams with his brothers, which did not go over well.

I can tell you from experience that everyone will not be for you or happy for you. During the journey of becoming what God called us to do, there will be bumps in the road. Let me encourage you today though dear friend, if God has called you to something, rest assured that the funds will be there.

Joseph faced many obstacles on his journey to becoming the prince of Egypt, but God provided for him the whole way. Just like this passage of scriptures I have shared today, no matter where Joseph was on his journey, God gave him favor and everything he put his hand to prospered. What a promise for His children, even in our world today.

Prayer:
Dear God, help me to keep the course you have laid out for me. Help me to not quit when the path gets rocky. Help me to look to your Word and find these Bible truths, just like this story of Joseph. If you called me to it, then I will have the strength and knowledge to prosper in the work. I may not be thrown into prison, but I have fought the enemy of my soul, many times. I know if you call me to a work, I will prosper.

Call to Action:

Do you feel like God has given you dreams and has nudged you in a certain area?

_____

_____

_____

_____

_____

_____

_____

_____

_____

_____

_____

_____

_____

_____

_____

_____

_____

_____

Write those dreams down, also write what you feel like would be your biggest wall.

_____

_____

_____

_____

_____

_____

_____

_____

_____

_____

_____

_____

_____

_____

_____

_____

_____

Day 15

Leviticus 26:3–5

3 If ye walk in my statutes, and keep my commandments, and do them; 4 Then I will give you rain in due season, and the land shall yield her increase, and the trees of the field shall yield their fruit. 5 And your threshing shall reach unto the vintage, and the vintage shall reach unto the sowing time: and ye shall eat your bread to the full, and dwell in your land safely.

What a wonderful promise! If we will walk in His statutes (keep His covenant) and keep His commandments, we will eat our bread to the full.

Our previous lessons in this devotional show that being prosperous is really in our hands. Already we have studied scriptures that point to our actions. It seems, without a doubt, God wants to bless His people. Not only does He want to, He delights in rewarding our dedication to seeking His ways.

In the Bible days, especially in the Old Testament, it was of great importance to own land, not only to own it but for God to bless it beyond the norm. They simply only needed to be obedient to His commandments.

We remember the kindness that David showed to Mephibosheth (2 Samuel). A promise to always sit at the King's table. But even more than that, his land was restored unto him, that he rightfully inherited.

Let us expect God to restore what belongs to us.

Prayer:
Lord, help me to seek to please you. Help me to know the path that I am to take. I want rain in due season. I want my land (my calling, my work) to yield an increase. I want to eat the fruit of my labor for you. I will obey your voice. I will obey your instructions, because I want to prosper in every area of my life. I don't want to ever lose sight of your purpose for me, no matter what it is that you have called me to do.

Call to Action:

Write down any thoughts that you feel like God is dealing with you about. Is there a place that you feel like you can do better? What is it?

_____

_____

_____

_____

_____

_____

_____

_____

_____

_____

_____

_____

_____

_____

_____

_____

_____

What can you do today to possibly help yourself to adjust your call?

_____

_____

_____

_____

_____

_____

_____

_____

_____

_____

_____

_____

_____

_____

_____

_____

_____

Day 16

1 Kings 2:1–3

1 Now the days of David drew nigh that he should die; and he charged Solomon his son, saying, 2 I go the way of all the earth: be thou strong therefore, and shew thyself a man; 3 And keep the charge of the LORD thy God, to walk in his ways, to keep his statutes, and his commandments, and his judgments, and his testimonies, as it is written in the law of Moses, that thou mayest prosper in all that thou doest, and whithersoever thou turnest thyself:

David is dying, so he is charging Solomon to be strong and show himself a man. What a charge to be given.

This is another passage of scripture that is letting us know that our prosperity is in our hands. We are to keep His judgments. On the website Beyond Today it states, "judgments are decisions handed down by judges to explain, broaden or narrow the application of existing law."

God's judgments illustrate how righteous decisions should be made. David is telling Solomon to be fair in his decisions, to be a person of integrity because his life would be a testimony. Isn't that what God is truly asking us to do? To be strong and show ourselves to be men and women of integrity, which will bring prosperity into our endeavors.

No matter which way we turn, we can be blessed by obeying these simple truths.

Prayer:
Father, help me to be strong. Help me to show myself as a man or woman. Help me to keep your judgments and be fair in all my actions when dealing with other people. Let me show integrity in my walk with you. Let me show wisdom when I need to portray it. Let me live the life pleasing to you that my testimony won't be tainted. I truly want to prosper in all my endeavors. I want to show my brothers and sisters in the family of God, that God is the God He says He is.

Call to Action:

If you were instructing a loved one, as you were leaving this world, what would you want them to hear the most? Do you feel like you have a good testimony to impart to them?

_____

_____

_____

_____

_____

_____

_____

_____

_____

_____

_____

_____

_____

_____

_____

_____

_____

_____

Have you seen God's prosperity from doing these acts?

_____

_____

_____

_____

_____

_____

_____

_____

_____

_____

_____

_____

_____

_____

_____

Day 17

Philippians 4:19

But my God shall supply all your need according to his riches in glory by Christ Jesus.

What a powerful message all wrapped up in a little Bible verse. *Shall, all,* and *riches* are like big handles of faith that a person can hold on too.

We know this verse can be found on many plaques, cards, and even painted on walls. Why? Because it's a solid promise with no strings attached. I love the "my God" part. That makes it extremely personal. Notice that the need is not plural. Just like the "Blessing maketh rich" not "the blessings." Everything a person needs to be prosperous is in this verse.

Psalm 50:10 says, "For every beast of the forest is mine, and the cattle upon a thousand hills." God was testifying against Israel for their sacrifices. He was letting them know He owns it all.

God's nature is to bless and supply our need. I don't know about you, but I want the Lord to help me in times of great need.

Prayer:
Heavenly Father, I am in NEED of you. I know that I can ask and receive. You take pleasure in blessing me. In this verse you speak of your riches. 'Riches' is plural, which means you have many blessings for me. I want to give thanks for how you have supplied all my need. You have helped me beyond even the natural needs. My greatest need is more of you. I will pursue you first and foremost, because nothing else matters if you are not number one in my life. I will forever give you the glory for every way that has been made for me and my family.

Call to Action:

What is your greatest need today? If you have several, write them all down. Don't be afraid to ask God to supply your need and some of your wants too.

_____

_____

_____

_____

_____

_____

_____

_____

_____

_____

_____

_____

_____

_____

_____

_____

_____

_____

Is there something you would like to give back to God that could help others?

_____

_____

_____

_____

_____

_____

_____

_____

_____

_____

_____

_____

_____

_____

_____

Day 18
1 Chronicles 22:11–13

11 Now, my son, the LORD be with thee; and prosper thou, and build the house of the LORD thy God, as he hath said of thee. 12 Only the LORD give thee wisdom and understanding, and give thee charge concerning Israel, that thou mayest keep the law of the LORD thy God. 13 Then shalt thou prosper, if thou takest heed to fulfil the statutes and judgments which the LORD charged Moses with concerning Israel: be strong, and of good courage; dread not, nor be dismayed.

The story of David wanting to build a house unto the Lord is quite a unique one. He was given the okay, then was told that he couldn't be the one to do it. We won't dwell on that part of the story too much. He had shed much blood and was a man of war, so this great feat was passed on to David's son, Solomon.

It's almost like rereading Joshua 1:7. David is imparting words of wisdom to Solomon on the success of this building. He is passing down the ingredients to a prosperous journey. He reminds Solomon that Moses is dead and if he will take heed to fulfil the statutes and judgments that have been passed down concerning Israel, he would prosper. He tells his son to be strong and of good courage. Truly it's our blueprint as well.

Every day we are building and working for God, spiritually and physically. We will see the work of our hands prosper when we lean on God and not ourselves.

Prayer:
Dear Heavenly Father, I am seeking you with all my heart. I long to build something for you. I long to make a difference in this life. I long to build a lasting memory for the work of God. I see through the scriptures that you have given us a road map to follow that will cause what we do to prosper. Thank you for every door that has been opened for me. Thank you for the way that has been made through standing on your word. I declare today that I am prospering in your Kingdom.

Call to Action:

What would the work of God look like for you today if everything was provided like it was for Solomon?

_____

_____

_____

_____

_____

_____

_____

_____

_____

_____

_____

_____

_____

_____

_____

_____

_____

_____

Do you believe that you could prosper in it by using God's word?

_____

_____

_____

_____

_____

_____

_____

_____

_____

_____

_____

_____

_____

_____

_____

Day 19
2 Chronicles 20:20

And they rose early in the morning, and went forth into the wilderness of Tekoa: and as they went forth, Jehoshaphat stood and said, Hear me, O Judah, and ye inhabitants of Jerusalem; Believe in the LORD your God, so shall ye be established; believe his prophets, so shall ye prosper.

There is a whole story in this chapter that can be helpful in understanding the full revelation of how listening to God's prophets can bring prosperity.

To summarize this individual verse, let's look at the context. Jehoshaphat is surrounded by several armies that far exceed the number of people Jehoshaphat has. But he knew where his help would come from. Setting his face toward seeking God, Jehoshaphat got the reassurance he needed.

God let the prophet rise up in the midst of those that began to declare the victory for Jehoshaphat. As the decree went forth, Jehoshaphat relays the message, but also lets them know they will prosper if they hearken to the word of the prophet.

It gives me great encouragement today that I can be obedient to God's ways and God's leaders and prosper in all of my ways.

Prayer:
God, I want to be sensitive to your men and women of God. I want to have a heart that is tender. Let my ears hear what you have to say. The enemy of this world is great but God, you are greater. Jehoshaphat said earlier in this chapter, that his eyes were on the Lord. My eyes are on you, as well, Father. Give me direction that I can prosper in all my ways. This passage may be speaking on a battle between armies, but I see that listening to wisdom and knowledge is a big key to prosperity.

Call to Action:

Are you facing a financial battle? Do you feel like God is giving you instructions?

_____

_____

_____

_____

_____

_____

_____

_____

_____

_____

_____

_____

_____

_____

_____

_____

_____

_____

Is He speaking through the prophet to you? Do you see a way out?

_____

_____

_____

_____

_____

_____

_____

_____

_____

_____

_____

_____

_____

_____

_____

_____

Day 20

2 Chronicles 26:3–5

3 Sixteen years old was Uzziah when he began to reign, and he reigned fifty and two years in Jerusalem. His mother's name also was Jecoliah of Jerusalem. 4 And he did that which was right in the sight of the LORD, according to all that his father Amaziah did. 5 And he sought God in the days of Zechariah, who had understanding in the visions of God: and as long as he sought the LORD, God made him to prosper.

God made Uzziah to prosper. What a statement! As long as he sought the Lord, he prospered. We should seek the Lord daily.

Can you imagine reigning over a country at 16 years old? Apparently, he did well. I'm sure he had some elders teaching him, one probably being his mother. He did right in the sight of the Lord. More than likely, Uzziah was a fair and trustworthy ruler. The scripture shares that the young king understood visions from God.

Many scriptures show us how to prosper. Many are tied to actions, like the action of leaning on God more than our flesh. No doubt, through seeking the Lord, he made the right decisions.

In the Bible days, prospering was a sign of being obedient. Prospering meant both natural and spiritual prosperity. Plenty of goods and riches come with wisdom and knowledge.

Prayer:
Dear heavenly Father, show me what seeking you looks like. Show me how to line up to the Word and seek after wisdom and knowledge. I want to prosper in all my ways. I want to understand visions. I want to know what is right in your sight. Show me how to prosper in your Kingdom. If I lack in any area, let me seek you to find the right path. The path that will lead me to prosperity, not for my gain, but that I can help others on their journey as well.

Call to Action:

If you were put over a country at 16 years old, what would be your first response?

_____

_____

_____

_____

_____

_____

_____

_____

_____

_____

_____

_____

_____

_____

_____

_____

_____

_____

_____

What would be the one thing that you would ask God to help you with?

_____

_____

_____

_____

_____

_____

_____

_____

_____

_____

_____

_____

_____

_____

_____

_____

_____

Day 21

2 Chronicles 31:20–21

20 And thus did Hezekiah throughout all Judah, and wrought that which was good and right and truth before the LORD his God. 21 And in every work that he began in the service of the house of God, and in the law, and in the commandments, to seek his God, he did it with all his heart, and prospered.

"It's a heart thing."

How many times have we heard that statement? We are not talking about that muscle that pumps blood through your body, but the heart of the soul, the mind, the spirit. The heart is the emotional part of our humanness. It's that gut feeling when something doesn't feel right, yes, that heart. When we work for God, we should always bring our best.

I would say no matter what you do in life, do it with all thine heart and you will see amazing results, whether it be natural or spiritual. Hezekiah did what was good and right. See the pattern in the last few devotionals. Do good, do right, seek God and whatever you do, do it with all thine heart, toward God and watch him prosper you.

Our life doesn't have to lack any good thing. When we bring our best to God and our heart is sincere the rewards will be seen by us and others.

Prayer:
God, the Word tells me my heart is deceitful and desperately wicked. I want to commit my motives unto you. Check me, God, for false feelings. Check my actions. Let me do all that I do for your glory. When you get glory, our flesh sometimes has to suffer. Most of the time, our hearts will tell on us. Our hearts are revealed in our everyday interactions with our fellow man. If my heart strays from your ways, then prick it, God. Show me my error, that I can correct it, that I may be blessed and prosperous.

Call to Action:

Do you ever wonder about your heart? Is it truly being truthful with God?

_____

_____

_____

_____

_____

_____

_____

_____

_____

_____

_____

_____

_____

_____

_____

_____

_____

_____

What is something you can do with all your heart to move God's hand in your life?

_____

_____

_____

_____

_____

_____

_____

_____

_____

_____

_____

_____

_____

_____

_____

_____

Day 22
Psalm 1:1–3

1 Blessed is the man that walketh not in the counsel of the ungodly, nor standeth in the way of sinners, nor sitteth in the seat of the scornful. 2 But his delight is in the law of the LORD; and in his law doth he meditate day and night. 3 And he shall be like a tree planted by the rivers of water, that bringeth forth his fruit in his season; his leaf also shall not wither; and whatsoever he doeth shall prosper.

Delight is a simple word, to take great pleasure in something. Meditate means plan mentally or to consider. The formula to prosperity is simple. But it's not easy. We have to be intentional about getting into the Word of God. We have to be intentional about meditating. It doesn't just happen.

One cannot delight themselves in the Word if they do not know it or read it. Can I encourage you today to learn the Bible? If you have a hard time reading it, you may find it easier to read inspirational books loaded with scriptures. That is how I trained myself to read and learn the scriptures. I'm a big fan of YouTube as well, where you can listen to the Bible audibly for free. You can also find great books that are loaded with Bible principles on YouTube.

When you get the Word in your heart, your spiritual life will take root, which becomes like that tree planted by the river, and its water source never runs dry. A well-watered tree will bring its fruit or leaves in due season, which simply means it will prosper. You can prosper, dear friend, by learning God's Word and putting it in your heart.

Prayer:
Heavenly Father, help me to hide your Word in my heart. Help me to be intentional about learning your Word, so that I can be like that tree planted by the river, where it's source of life never dries up. I must know your Word to delight in it. I must know your Word to meditate on it. Give me a deep desire to glean from the Bible like never before. So many passages point to blessings and prosperity through knowing the Word. I will start reading at least a couple of encouraging scriptures everyday. I will be intentional about finding ways to put it in my heart.

Call to Action:

What will you do today that will help you get more scriptures in your mind?

_____

_____

_____

_____

_____

_____

_____

_____

_____

_____

_____

_____

_____

_____

_____

_____

_____

_____

What do you think of when you hear the word *delight*?

_____

_____

_____

_____

_____

_____

_____

_____

_____

_____

_____

_____

_____

_____

_____

_____

Day 23
Psalm 68:19

Blessed be the Lord, who daily loadeth us with benefits, even the God of our salvation. Selah

When I think of benefits I think of insurance, I think of 401k savings, etc. It's like a bonus for your participation in a system.

In the world's package, you pay extra for extra benefits. The benefits that come with some insurance are out of this world. People will quit jobs to go to other jobs where the benefits are better. The Lord gives His benefits to us daily. These benefits from God can't be measured by man.

Every day that I wake up in my right mind, it's because of Him. Every day that I can see, touch, feel, and even walk, it's because of Him. Truly, He has the ultimate benefit package. We simply live a righteous and holy life and He comes through with pay offs every day.

Our God is so good that He will even bless you when you know you really weren't being all you could be. That's like an earthly parent, still loving, still providing, even after a child has left home. We can't really grasp His benefits, but the Word assures us that He has them for us.

Prayer:
Lord, your benefits are beyond my feeble little mind. My humanness can't fathom the benefits you have for me. Help me to stand on your promises. Help me to expect the goodness of God. Your Word doesn't lie. In this passage, you really don't pinpoint the benefits that you give us daily. We as your children have to see your hands in our everyday life. I love your promise in this verse because there are no guidelines for you to load me daily with benefits. You have proven your goodness over and over in my life, and I thank you for allowing me to prosper/benefit through your biblical principles in the mighty name of Jesus.

Call to Action:

Can you see God's hand in your life, on a daily basis?

_____

_____

_____

_____

_____

_____

_____

_____

_____

_____

_____

_____

_____

_____

_____

_____

_____

_____

_____

What benefits do you see God bringing into your life daily?

_____

_____

_____

_____

_____

_____

_____

_____

_____

_____

_____

_____

_____

_____

_____

_____

_____

Day 24
Psalm 92:12–14

12 The righteous shall flourish like the palm tree: he shall grow like a cedar in Lebanon. 13 Those that be planted in the house of the LORD shall flourish in the courts of our God. 14 They shall still bring forth fruit in old age; they shall be fat and flourishing;

Flourishing, to me, is just another word for prospering. I like to look up the things that the Bible uses for metaphors, like palm trees. The palm trees had many uses in Bible days. One thing about the palm tree: it is upright and it towers into the sky. It has a beauty of its own. Also, its leaves were used to make baskets, roofs, etc.

The palm tree is very rich in its own way. The fruit it produces is a nutritious fruit. It's no secret that people are compared to trees a lot in the scriptures. The cedar trees of Lebanon can grow up to 120-feet tall, which means the roots grow extremely deep. The cedar tree is known for its height and its beauty, as well.

The comparison in this passage is showing the strength, the beauty and the tallness of these particular trees and comparing them to our walk, our blessings. "Fat and flourishing" is symbolic to our blessing, our prosperity, if you will.

Prayer:
God, I love the way you compare me to your beautiful creation. Trees are beautiful to look at. You made so many trees to give fruit, which means they can sustain someone. Help me to give off the fruit that I'm supposed to give. Your Word tells me that I'm flourishing like the palm tree. Help me realize when you are working behind the scenes in my life, that you are adding blessings to my life, so that I will in return bless others. My life is flourishing like the palm tree and growing like the cedars in Lebanon. Thank you for enriching my life with prosperity beyond this world's view of prosperity.

Call to Action:

Why do you think God compares us to trees so often in the Bible?

_____

_____

_____

_____

_____

_____

_____

_____

_____

_____

_____

_____

_____

_____

_____

_____

What kind of tree do you think that you would be compared to and why?

_____

_____

_____

_____

_____

_____

_____

_____

_____

_____

_____

_____

_____

_____

_____

_____

_____

Day 25

Proverbs 3:9–10

9 Honour the LORD with thy substance, and with the firstfruits of all thine increase: 10 So shall thy barns be filled with plenty, and thy presses shall burst out with new wine.

Honour can mean to fulfill (an obligation) or keep (an agreement).

In other words, we need to give God our time, money, love, and most of all commitment. When you honor someone you also respect their place, their calling, or position. The "firstfruits" in the Bible were considered tithes. A tenth of your wages or even your increase was to be given to God (the church) first. This could be wages, livestock, even harvest from crops. When you would give your tithes, (your obligation, your agreement) you opened up an avenue to where God could give back to you.

This passage speaks of barns, which is harvest. The barns will be full, not lacking. The presses would be bursting with new wine. I love God's multiplication. You give 10% and He gives back 100-fold.

Notice even after giving of their substance, their barns and presses were full to the brim. It doesn't take much to stand in the blessings of God or to prosper in His Kingdom. Just honor Him, give to Him freely, and watch Him run you over with blessings.

Prayer:
God, I am so thankful for your giving formula. You are the only one that will give 100-fold back for just 10%. I love how you want to bless your people. I love how you speak to me and show me how to give back to you. Because when I do this simple act of obedience, you go above and beyond anything I can imagine. I am so humbled by your generosity. You truly want to prosper me. You show this act by teaching me through your Word how to be abundantly blessed. I give you all the honor and praise this day in the mighty name of Jesus.

Call to Action:

What do you think *honour* means in this passage?

_____

_____

_____

_____

_____

_____

_____

_____

_____

_____

_____

_____

_____

_____

_____

_____

_____

_____

_____

What can you do to honor God besides give money? Can you see His hands in your life through giving?

_____

_____

_____

_____

_____

_____

_____

_____

_____

_____

_____

_____

_____

_____

_____

_____

Day 26
Proverbs 11:24–25

24 There is that scattereth, and yet increaseth; and there is that withholdeth more than is meet, but it tendeth to poverty. **25** The liberal soul shall be made fat: and he that watereth shall be watered also himself.

There is a common theme through this devotional: give and it shall be given back to you.

Look at verse 24, when you scattereth, when you sow, your seed will increase. Yet, if you withhold more than you need, even what you have will tendeth to poverty. In other words, you will lack. You can have a good harvest, but if you don't give graciously to God of your substance, you will still want for His blessings.

The liberal soul—the person that gives freely, a cheerful giver, the one that gives more than required—will be made fat. Not fat in our physical bodies, but fat with the riches of God. These riches can't be measured by man. They're not always monetary.

The true riches of God are joy, peace, and strength. But this passage also lets us know that if we will water, give of our substance, we will be watered as well. Water to a plant can mean its very existence. So give abundantly that you can see God's prosperity in your life.

Prayer:
Dear God, you have shown me how to be blessed. Please nudge me in my spirit when I need to give more than I'm giving. Thank you for revealing the path to blessings and prosperity. Thank you for loving me so much that you have filled your Holy Word with scripture after scripture of revelation. I ask you to light a fire inside of me that burns so hot that it will not be quenched until I pick up the Word of God and consume the message of reaping and sowing. I decree today that I'm scattering seeds that will come back to me abundantly. Thank you, God, for your formula of how to be blessed.

Call to Action:

Have you ever felt God nudge you to give something of value away, and when you did he gave back way more? Write down a time this happened, who you gave to, etc., and how it came back.

_____

_____

_____

_____

_____

_____

_____

_____

_____

_____

_____

_____

_____

_____

_____

_____

_____

_____

What can you sow today besides money? Write down some areas that you can sow from.

_____

_____

_____

_____

_____

_____

_____

_____

_____

_____

_____

_____

_____

_____

_____

_____

_____

Day 27

Jeremiah 29:11

For I know the thoughts that I think toward you, saith the LORD, thoughts of peace, and not of evil, to give you an expected end.

This scripture is probably one of the most quoted verses from this era. At the time this verse was penned, the children of Israel were in captivity. What a consolation to know that even in the midst of our problems or even heartache that God is making a way for us.

We quote Bible verses sometimes because they sound good or they fit our situation at that moment. We will take scripture out of context to soothe our souls. We should always read the context in whole.

This particular passage is truly an eye-opening story. God tells the children of Israel to build houses, plant vine-yards, and reap their harvest, even in the midst of captivity. They were in captivity for 70 years! We know from God's Word that the life expectancy of humans is around 70 years. I often compared that time frame with the 70 years of captivity in Babylon.

Our estimated time in our fleshly realm lets us know that we are in bondage to this flesh until God calls us home. But He tells us to build, to plant, to reap our harvests while we are here. His plan is to bring us to our expected end.

Prayer:
God, I know that you care so much for me. I know that you are there at all times. I want to thank you for blessing me even in the hard times. That even when I'm in the midst of a valley or storm that your plans are to prosper me. I need you to give me the courage and strength to wait on my expected end. I love how you always go before us. How you always show us through your Word how we can stand strong and look for your hand throughout our journey called life. I love you, because you first loved me. And I give you all the glory, in the precious name of Jesus.

Call to Action:

Did you know that the children of Israel were in captivity when God shared this wonderful promise? If you didn't know this biblical truth, how do you feel about it now?

_____

_____

_____

_____

_____

_____

_____

_____

_____

_____

_____

_____

_____

_____

_____

_____

_____

Can you name some times that God prospered you even in the midst of a trial?

_____

_____

_____

_____

_____

_____

_____

_____

_____

_____

_____

_____

_____

_____

_____

_____

_____

Day 28
Malachi 3:10

Bring ye all the tithes into the storehouse, that there
may be meat in mine house, and prove me now here-
with, saith the LORD of hosts, if I will not open you the
windows of heaven, and pour you out a blessing, that
there shall not be room enough to receive it.

This Old Testament scripture has been debated for hundreds of years. Do we pay tithes or do we not? I don't seek to answer this question for you, but I will share my insight and results from obeying this scripture.

This verse is one of the only places we find in the Bible where God says, "prove Me now." We find in many scriptures about prosperity that when we do the things that God is requiring us to do, the windows of heaven will open up over our lives.

Many verses in Malachi 3 show us benefits from doing this act of faith. God will always give back more than we give. So why wouldn't we want to give our tithes into the store house/church? God says He will rebuke the devourer for our sake.

I don't have enough room here to dissect this passage, but there is an abundance of revelation in this reading today. You can expect prosperity to come to you from the harvest of good seed that you have sown. He will give you more than you can contain.

Prayer:
Oh God, I love how you teach me to prosper. I live under an open heaven. I know that life happens to us all. I don't always see the blessings until they are manifested in my life. I know that you teach me to ask. But you also show me ways to have prosperity through your precious Word. I want to show you that I love you and believe in Bible principals by giving my tithes and offerings unto the work of God. You are a good, good Father and your hand is always open to me to give me the provision that you have promised to your children.

Call to Action:

Have you ever proved God? Have you ever given up something out of obedience and God showed himself faithful?

_____

_____

_____

_____

_____

_____

_____

_____

_____

_____

_____

_____

_____

_____

_____

_____

_____

_____

What does an open window from heaven mean to you?

_____

_____

_____

_____

_____

_____

_____

_____

_____

_____

_____

_____

_____

_____

_____

_____

Day 29

2 Corinthians 9:6–7

6 But this I say, He which soweth sparingly shall reap also sparingly; and he which soweth bountifully shall reap also bountifully. 7 Every man according as he purposeth in his heart, so let him give; not grudgingly, or of necessity: for God loveth a cheerful giver.

Throughout our study of prosperity in the Bible, we see the law of harvest. It is simply sowing and reaping. God magnifies giving. We can give of our money, our time, our love and even of our substance.

The simplicity of God's blessings is really in your hands. Many times we may look at others being blessed and wonder where God is in our life. Now let me stop and say that sometimes God will let us give and give and give, I've been there, and we may even question where the harvest is. One thing we can stand on is His Word. It doesn't lie. It may not come when you want it, but it will come right on time.

Let us sow bountifully so that we can reap bountifully. If we sow sparingly then that is the harvest we will get. Some people are natural givers, some are not. Verse 7 says that we should decide what we are going to give and do it cheerfully. To give cheerfully means readily and willingly.

My dear friends I challenge you today to cheerfully start sowing seeds of abundance that you can reap in abundance. Prosperity is for you. It's God's plan for us.

Prayer:

God, I am coming to you today asking you to show me how to be a cheerful giver. I pray that you place an undeniable desire in my spirit to give abundantly. I have been challenged through reading this devotional to look at my life and see where I stand in being blessed and prosperous. I have read for myself that if I give, it will be given back to me. I thank you for all the examples through the Bible that truly show me how to be prosperous. Prosperity is not necessarily how much money a person has, but your Word confirms that you want your children to prosper. Today, I give you the highest praise for all your blessings on me and my family. In Jesus name, let it be so.

Call to Action:

Have you ever read these scriptures and acted on them? What is something that you can give today in abundance that you can reap a harvest from?

_____

_____

_____

_____

_____

_____

_____

_____

_____

_____

_____

_____

_____

_____

_____

_____

_____

What would you like God to give back to you today?

_____

_____

_____

_____

_____

_____

_____

_____

_____

_____

_____

_____

_____

_____

_____

_____

Day 30
Luke 6:38

Give, and it shall be given unto you; good measure, pressed down, and shaken together, and running over, shall men give into your bosom. For with the same measure that ye mete withal it shall be measured to you again.

I intentionally saved our last two days of scripture for the ending of this 31-day devotional. Even though there is one more to reflect on, this verse alone could have a whole book by itself.

We can decree and declare this scripture over our lives and watch God literally move in these promises. My dear reader, this is not a suggestion. This is an imperative statement, a statement that will forever be true.

What I want to ask you today is, what are you giving? Money, time, and love are just a few things we can give. Notice how it says men will give unto you. Why, you may ask. Because when you give you are pretty much giving unto man.

This giving goes beyond our tithes and offerings. When you are asked to help with a project at the church you attend or even the community you live in, that is an opportunity to give.

Have you ever put some clothes in a bag and you just kept pressing down and adding more to it? Think about God giving back to you like that. Pressed down and running over. Whatever you "mete out" will come back to you. Luke 6:38 is a message for God to prosper you in so many ways.

Prayer:
God, show me how to benefit from this promise. Show me ways to give of myself, whatever that may be. You have filled the Bible with instructions on how to be prosperous. I do want to see prosperity in my life, but not for selfish gain. I want to give to those in need. I want to pay for someone's groceries in the check out line. I want to buy a car for a family that needs transportation. I want to purchase someone's plane ticket to go to a conference or even a few days of relaxation. God, I have been the person in need many times, and you have always come through. I thank you for these insightful passages that let me know how to be blessed.

123

Call to Action:

Have you ever given something of great value to someone because God laid it on your heart?

_____

_____

_____

_____

_____

_____

_____

_____

_____

_____

_____

_____

_____

_____

_____

_____

Have you ever proven this scripture to be true? What did you give and what did God give back?

_____

_____

_____

_____

_____

_____

_____

_____

_____

_____

_____

_____

_____

_____

_____

_____

Day 31

Ephesians 3:20

Now unto him that is able to do exceeding abundantly above all that we ask or think, according to the power that worketh in us.

Last but definitely not least. I mentioned in the last devotion that I purposely saved these two for last.

We all imagine in our minds a more prosperous life from time to time. We all sometimes have to ask God to move in our finances. You may have asked God to help you purchase a car, house, etc. This verse tells us that He is well "able to do exceeding abundantly above all we could ask or think."

There is a famous quote by Albert Einstein, that "imagination is everything." It is the preview of life's coming attractions. Here is the key to unlock this promise in our life: the last eight words in this verse hold our future in them.

When the power of God is working in our life, in our spirit, in our hearts then we can expect God to bring these biblical principles to pass. His word is powerful, and if His word is in us then we have the power of God working in us.

What are we asking God for today, what are we believing for? It's okay to want God to bless you and prosper you. It's His good pleasure to give unto us.

Prayer:
My provider, my God in whom I trust, I ask today for blessings beyond my imagination. Show me how to have the power of God working in me, that I can walk in this promise of abundant provision. What an amazing insight that you have revealed to me. Thank you for letting me know that you blessed me with a mind to think beyond the norm. Thank you for revealing this simple Bible verse, to show me that you truly are a loving and giving Father and you desire to give me exceedly abundantly more than I could ask or think. We give you all the glory in Jesus' name. Amen.

Call to Action:

What have you asked God for lately, that maybe you think is
way out there?

_____

_____

_____

_____

_____

_____

_____

_____

_____

_____

_____

_____

_____

_____

_____

_____

_____

I challenge you today to take off the limits and ask BIG. Go ahead, write down all of the things you'd like to see in your life but think are impossible and see what God will do.

_____

_____

_____

_____

_____

_____

_____

_____

_____

_____

_____

_____

_____

_____

_____

_____

www.ingramcontent.com/pod-product-compliance
Lightning Source LLC
Chambersburg PA
CBHW051732040426
42447CB00008B/1092